www.dinobibi.com

Author: Celia Jenkins
Editor: Kristy Elam
Illustrator: Teena Rahim

© Copyright 2019 - Dinobibi: All rights reserved. No part of this publication may be reproduced, stored in retrieval systems, or transmitted by any means, including electronic, mechanical, photocopying, or otherwise, without prior written permission of the publisher and copyright holder. **Disclaimer:** Although the author and Dinobibi have taken all reasonable care in preparing this book, we make no warranty about the accuracy or completeness of its content and, to the maximum extent permitted, disclaim all liability arising from its use.

CONTENTS

Introduction (pg. 4)

Geography of China (pg. 10)

Weather in China (pg. 14)

History of China (pg. 18)

Native Plants & Animals (pg. 22)

Food, Culture, & Traditions (pg. 26)

Famous People (pg. 37)

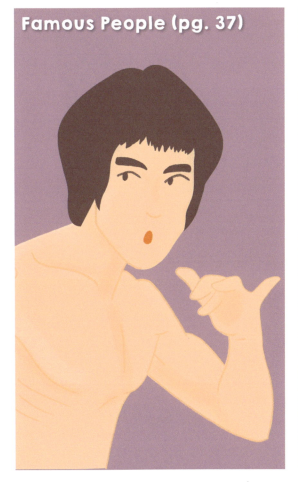

Major Cities & Attractions (pg. 40)

INTRODUCTION: HELLO FRIENDS!

Nǐ hǎo, or hello! My name is Ping Chen. My first name is Chen; it means great! Ping, my surname, or last name, is one of the most popular names in China, and it means apple.

If Chinese children study English, they usually pick an English name to use in class, and a lot of my friends chose the name Apple. I'm a boy, but many girls choose the name Apple, too.

I wanted to be more unique, so I chose the name Ringo, like Ringo Starr, who was from The Beatles. My Mum loves The Beatles. It's a funny coincidence because in Japanese 'ringo' means apple! But you can call me Chen.

I live in China in a province called Zhejiang, which is on the East Coast of China. We can go to the East China Sea, but it's still a long way to travel, so we don't go there often.

I like Zhejiang province because it's more developed than other places in China. Just a few decades ago, Zhejiang was full of farms and fishing villages.

However, it has become one of the richest and most developed provinces in China. But I don't live in a big city; I live in Lishui, which is one of the biggest districts in Zhejiang but with one of the smallest populations.

Cheng Huang temple in the background of Hangzhou West Lake and city

Lishui means 'beautiful water,' and we have a lot of lakes and rivers in the town. My town is such a peaceful place to live, better than a big city! I like to go fishing with my grandpa, who I call Yéyé, on the weekends. I spend a lot of time with my grandpa and grandma (I call her Nǎinai) because my parents work away from home a lot. My mother is an English teacher; she works at a big school in Hangzhou City which is three or four hours away by car. Hangzhou is the biggest city in Zhejiang with over 6 million people living there.

My mother usually comes home on the weekends or for holidays. We speak every day on the phone, though.

My father is an architect. He has a good business in Zhejiang because so many companies want to build big skyscrapers. My father works from home when he can, so I see him more often. But if he is overseeing a big project, he works away for several days at a time.

He does a lot of projects in Hangzhou City. He also travels to Suzhou, in Jiangsu province, because they have a lot of development there, too.

My Yéyé is so amazed that Bàbà (that's my Dad) studied hard and became an architect. Yéyé didn't go to school for many years, so he couldn't be an architect. He worked hard his whole life as a builder.

He did a lot of things with timber, because in Lishui we have so many forests and trees. Now he's retired and enjoys going fishing every day. He also goes to the temple with Nǎinai, as both of my grandparents are Chinese Buddhists. The temple they go to is very popular, the walls around it are painted bright orange, and you can smell the sweet incense before you walk into the courtyard.

Fun Fact:
There are around 250 million Buddhists in China.

My parents are atheists, but sometimes they go to the temple as well. In China, it's usual for people to go to religious places, even if they don't believe it.

Chinese Buddhism is different to other types of Buddhism, we also believe in Chinese folk stories, Confucianism, and Taoism. I'm not sure what I believe, but I think it's interesting, and religion is one of my favourite things to... study in school, but we don't do those lessons very often. At my school, the teachers are more interested in maths and science!

A lot of children go to my school; it's one of the biggest schools in Lishui. Our classes are big. My class has forty-six students in it, but some classes are much bigger than that. Forty-six students is too many for one teacher to control.

The naughty students have to sit at the back of the classroom, so they don't distract the good students. I sit on the second row at the front, which means I'm a really good student. In China, people are very competitive; we want to be the best. So I know I need to study hard and get good grades.

I'm lucky because Māmā (my mother) is a teacher, so she can help me with my English homework. Some schools in big cities have a foreign teacher who comes from America or the UK to help students learn English. My school is in a small town, so we don't have a foreign teacher, but my mother studied abroad so she helps me a lot.

My grandma never went to a university, but she helps me with my homework, too. I'm really lucky because I have a big family and everyone can help me. In China, some kids just live with their grandparents and never see their mother and father. I don't think this is so good. But I'd really like a brother or sister. China used to have strict rules about having a lot of children. Things are different now, so my parents can have another baby if they want to.

Pop Quiz!

Which of these is not a popular Chinese instrument?

1. The djembe
2. The erhu
3. The pipa

(Answer—1. The djembe is a skin-covered drum that comes from West Africa. The erhu is a Chinese stringed instrument that is over 1,000 years old, and the pipa is a four-stringed Chinese instrument that looks like a lute.)

Now I'm eleven and my birthday is coming up, so soon I will be leaving primary school and going to secondary school.

I know I need to study hard in school so that I can go to a university. In China, kids don't start school until they are six or seven. My mother told me that in the UK children go to school when they are four or five years old. So before I started school, my mother taught me at home to make sure I would be a smart boy. She taught me English and geography. We have a lot of maps around our house, and I like to plan where I'll travel to when I'm older.

My best subjects are English, religious studies, and geography. In China, maths and science are really important. I'm quite good at these, but I need to study more. I find history quite difficult because China has a very long history, and there are so many things to remember. But I can't be good at everything. I also study the piano, I have a lesson twice a week, and my Nǎinai makes me practice for forty-minutes every day. She's very strict about my piano practice... but sometimes Yéyé can persuade her that I should take a break, and I go fishing with him instead!

The secondary school in Lishui isn't the best in Zhejiang province, but I don't have a choice, I have to study hard and do my best. My father told me that I can achieve anything if I work hard. "Look at me, I was the son of a builder, and I didn't go to a good secondary school either. But I worked hard, and went to a university, and now I'm a popular architect!" my father told me, to inspire me to work hard. It worked, and now I always do my best!

Before we continue our trip, I would like to know more about you.
Can you please complete this little questionnaire for me?

Your name:

Which country are you from:

Who are you traveling with?

Which places in China are you most excited about? Why?

CHAPTER 1
GEOGRAPHY OF CHINA

Nǐ hǎo, it's me again. So here's the thing about China: it's one country, but not really. It's more like a lot of countries all squished together. The People's Republic of China (that's China's full name) is the fourth biggest country in the world, but it's made up of twenty-three provinces that are all so different to each other that they're basically like different places. People from different provinces don't even speak the same language! But I guess it's a bit like the United States of America. In America there are fifty states, and while they all speak English, those places can be quite different from each other, too.

I told you before that I live in Zhejiang Province. Just to give you an idea about how big a province is in China, Zhejiang has: 11 prefectures, 90 counties, and 1,570 townships.

There are a lot of things that Zhejiang is famous for. One thing is the beauty, but of course I'm bound to say that it's beautiful because I'm from here, and I love it!

Fun Fact:
The province with the biggest population is Guangdong. Over 100,000,000 people live there!

The population of the province is more than 57,000,000. How does that compare to where you live? I bet Zhejiang is bigger!

Hangzhou West Lake Longjing tea plantations

We're also famous for tea, and Hangzhou (where Māmā works) is sometimes called the 'tea capital of China.' In Hangzhou, they have a very popular type of green tea called Longjing which comes from a place called Dragon Well village. In the west, people don't always make green tea correctly: they use too many leaves, and boil it too long so that it becomes bitter and dark. Longjing is a very sweet, delicate taste and is known around the world.

China has different ethnic groups, and 91% of people are Han Chinese, like me. Other minorities like the Zhuang, Hui, Manchu, Uyghur, and Miao live more in the west of China, but Zhejiang Province is more than 99% Han Chinese. Some Han Chinese treat the minority people badly; they think that the Han should be in charge and take away the rights of other ethnic groups. I get really angry when people say Han are the best because we're the same as everyone else. Some minority people look different from us, but we're all Chinese at heart.

Shanghai skyline and cityscape at sunset

My best friend at school, Wang Jun, has a grandmother from Tibet, but I don't think he's any different from me. I think he's so lucky because sometimes he gets to visit Tibet in the holidays.

Do you know what the capital city of China is? Since 1949, Beijing has been the capital, although it was the capital in the past, too.

Fun Fact:
Aside from Beijing, the Four Great Ancient Capitals of China include Xi'an, Nanjing, and Luoyang.

Beijing was called Peking, and that's why we have a famous dish called 'Peking Duck.' Although Beijing is the capital, it's not the largest city in China. The largest is Shanghai, which has around 24 million people living there. I've only been to Beijing once, but we go to Shanghai every year. Our journey takes four or five hours to get there by car or train. I like going to Shanghai because it's so cosmopolitan. We never see foreigners in Lishui, but if we go to Shanghai and visit the People's Park or the famous Nanjing Road shopping street, we see many different people.

The longest river in not only China, but all of Asia, is the Yangtze River (Changjiang in Chinese), which is over 6,000km long. Some people say that the map of China looks like a chicken, and the Yangtze River is its wing.

Yangtze River

China's flag is known as the Five-Starred Red Flag, because it's plain red with one big yellow star and four small stars. Some people don't like our flag now, because red stands for the Communist Revolution which was a time when a lot of people died. The big star stands for the Chinese Communist Party, and the four small stars represent the people of China: the peasants, working class, the petite bourgeoisie (which means middle-class) and the national bourgeoisie (which means upper-class).

Currency in China

Something interesting about Chinese money is that our currency has two names. We use the Renminbi, which means the people's currency, and we use the symbol RMB. But most people call our money 'yuan,' which means the same thing and is a much older world. Actually, when you go into a shop, there's another word that people use, kuai, which a very common word and means exactly the same as renminbi and yuan, but it's the one people use most. They also use the word 'qian,' which means money. So if a shopkeeper wants to tell you something costs 10 yuan, they might say "10 kuai qian" which really translates as "10 pieces of money" Complicated, right?

China is an inexpensive place to live. Even in one of the big cities, a nice apartment is cheaper than in other countries. China is a developing country, which means people are poorer. A lot of things make a country 'developed,' and China doesn't have them all yet. For example, 97% of Chinese people have access to tap water, and around 95% of adults can read and write. In countries like Afghanistan, the Congo, and Nepal, most people don't have access to clean water, so we are more developed than those places. But if you look at other things, like how much money people earn, China still counts as a developing country because many people are poor and earn so little. A usual salary in China is 10,000 – 15,000 RMB per month.

Some jobs pay more than others, and a salary can go up and down depending on performance. For example, at my Māmā's school, the foreign teachers (from the UK or America) earn about 12,000 RMB a month, plus a bonus of 1,000 or 2,000. But Māmā only earns 6,000 or 7,000 RMB, with the potential for a bonus. This salary is actually better than some other teachers, even though she works in a city and can expect to be paid more. For my Bàbà, his job is highly skilled, and he works hard for a good company, so his salary is much higher. He usually earns 22,000 RMB per month, which is very high for someone in Lishui! Before my Yéyé retired, he only earned about 2,000 or 3,000 RMB per month, so he thinks Bàbà's salary is amazing!

The cost of living is low where we live, but because Māmā works in Hangzhou and rents a room there, we're not as rich as you might think. If we go out to a very cheap restaurant for lunch, we can get a small bowl of rice or noodles for under 10 RMB. But usually I choose something bigger, and it costs 15 or 18 RMB. If we go out to dinner and have a bigger meal, it might be 35 or 40 RMB. If we go to one of my favourite western restaurants in a big city, it can cost more than 100 RMB per person. That's for a treat only!

My grandparents don't have a car, so when Bàbà is away we travel by bicycle or public bus. The bus is just 2RMB for a short journey or 3RMB for a longer one. Năinai shops at the market and likes to get a good deal for things. If she buys a kilogram of fruit or vegetables, it can be less than 10RMB, and she always tries to get something in season. A big loaf of bread is about 15RMB, and milk is about the same price.

You can live for cheap if you know where to shop! In the big cities, there are fancy supermarkets where things cost double as much, or more! When it's just me and my grandparents, we eat simply and spend very little. Oh, and sometimes if Yéyé and I are really lucky, we catch a fish for our dinner!

CHAPTER 2
WEATHER IN CHINA

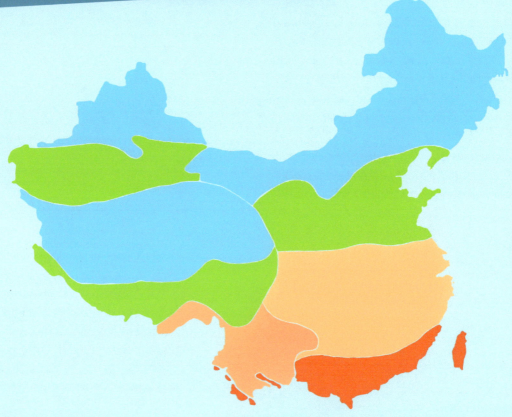

Phew, it's hot today! What's the weather like where you are? Did you know that the weather in China can be really extreme? The hottest weather we ever had in China happened in 2017. It was 50.5 °C (122.9 °F), but not in all of China, just in a place called Turpan in Xinjiang. The Turpan Depression is one of the hottest, driest places on Earth! The coldest weather ever recorded in China happened in 2009. This time, Inner Mongolia got hit by extreme weather. It was −58 °C (−72 °F). So if you compare the hottest and coldest weather we've ever had in this one, vast country, there's a difference of over 100 degrees!

If you look at an average temperature map for all of China, you can see how big the country is by how different the temperatures are. Down in the south, the map is a deep red: average temperatures are warm all year round, and you'll never need to wear a jacket! As you travel up to the middle, the colours change to orange, which means it's the sort of weather that's nice and warm in the daytime but cooler in the evening. As you continue north, and the country extends to the east and west, the colours change to pale orange, then white, then light blue, then darker and darker. In the dark blue places, the average temperature is cold enough to have snow! But further north, there are patches of orange again in Xinjiang. China has such a fascinating map, and I could look at it all day, even if it does look like a chicken!

Fun Fact:
In our capital, Beijing, the annual temperatures have an average range of -2 °C to 27 °C (28 °F to 81°F).

View of the Gaochang ruins near the city of Turpan, Xinjiang

In Zhejiang, our climate is humid and tropical. You might think that we have the same climate all over China, but the country is so big that the weather varies greatly.

In the south, weather is often sunny and tropical, but in the north, it's often cold with a lot of snow. In Lishui, we have hot summers and mild winters. Our average annual temperature is around 15 to 19 °C (which is 59 to 66 °F). To me, that's the perfect weather. You can just wear a t-shirt and shorts in the daytime, but it's not so hot that you're sweating buckets! The hottest it's ever been in Lishui, where I live, is about 35 °C, which is way too hot for me!

In the spring, we often get rain, and then it's even rainier towards the summer, but autumn and winter are drier. Actually, it's not just rain: in China we get typhoons. The typhoons come from the Pacific Ocean and can be really serious, and typhoons can cause floods. But that's not the only natural disaster we get in China. Like a lot of places in this part of the world, China is prone to earthquakes.

Sichuan earthquake

Fun Fact: The world's deadliest ever recorded earthquake happened in 1556, in central China.

If you look at the top ten deadliest natural disasters that have ever happened, five of them have been in China for many reasons. One reason is that China is a developing country, so our buildings aren't so good and are more likely to fall down if there is a natural disaster. Also, we have a large population, and a lot of these people are poor, which means that if something bad happens, many people need help. Unfortunately, doctors and nurses in China aren't always as good as in other places, so if a lot of people are hurt they can't help them, and there are too many people for the doctors to help.

It sounds bad, doesn't it? But things are changing. People in China are getting wealthier and living in better houses, which means that when disaster strikes, fewer people get hurt. Also, technological advances mean we know sooner if something is going to happen, and because we have radios, televisions and mobile phones, people can find out about what to do earlier.

For these reasons, I'm interested in geography, which isn't just about maps, topography (which means detailed features about a land), and inhabitants (which means the people who live there). Geography can really help people because the more we know about our world, the more we can do to look after it and look after each other. Sometimes I think when I grow up I'd like to be a professor of religious studies, but if I can't do that, then I'd like to do something with geography. A cartographer is someone who makes maps, a seismologist is someone who studies earthquakes, and a conservationist is someone who works to protect and preserve wildlife and the environment. All of those sound like really cool jobs to me.

Uh-oh, it's started raining. I hope Yéyé has his yǔsǎn (that means umbrella). He hates when it rains because it makes his hair go all frazzled and stand on end, and he looks like a mad inventor. But he also likes the rain because it makes the fish come to the surface at the lake. I wonder if I'll be having fish for dinner tonight?

> **Fun Fact**
>
> If you like warm daytime temperatures and cooler evenings, October is the best month to visit China. August is very hot and January is quite cool, but in October the temperatures are comfortably warm in the day and not too cold at night.

> **Fun Fact**
>
> For a single country, China has the largest climate differences. China has both very hot temperatures and very cold temperatures.

CHAPTER 3
HISTORY OF CHINA

Qin dynasty Terracotta Army

I've already told you that China has a long history. In fact, China has one of the oldest histories in the world. We've been around for a long time. History lessons at school are extra boring because there is so much for me to learn. Our written history started over 3,000 years ago, so you can imagine how much stuff I learn.

I was really surprised to hear that American history is so short. People have lived in America as long as people have lived in China, way back to the ancient civilizations. But until 400 or 500 years ago, just the Native Americans lived in America, who some people call the American Indians. In China, we have dynasties where different groups ruled the country. Our dynastic history goes way back, and China had dynasties before Europe had the Byzantine Empire, before Roman Empire, and before the Ancient Greeks, too. Just thinking about all that

The first ever dynasty in China was called the Xia Dynasty lasting from 2070 to 1600 BC, meaning it started 2070 years before Jesus Christ was born. But this dynasty was such along time ago that a lot of people think of it as mythology.

Unlike later dynasties, not muchevidence exists to tell us about the Xia times. In recent years, we have more evidence, likewhen they found the Terracotta Warriors, but I won't tell you about that yet. I'm getting ahead of myself!

Actually, the Xia Dynasty sounds like it lasted a long time, but compared to some of the later dynasties, it wasn't very long at all. Ancient history consisted of four different dynasties. Imperial history, which ran from 221 BC to 1912 AD, had different dynasties, but sometimes they ran at the same time because they controlled different areas. It's quite confusing!

Fun Fact:
The Terracotta Army is made up of over 8,000 soldiers, 670 horses, and 130 chariots.

In school, we spend time learning about the most important dynasties. We study the Qin Dynasty a lot because of a special artifact that comes from that time. Can you guess what it is? I'll give you a clue. The collection has thousands of pieces, and they were buried underground for a long, long time. They were made to protect a powerful Emperor in his afterlife. I'm referring to the Terracotta Warriors, also called the Terracotta Army.

Fun Fact:

In 1998, Yang Zhifa (one of the farmers who found the Terracotta Army) got to meet American President Bill Clinton

I've never been to Xi'an to see the warriors, but I hope to go one day. Qin Shi Huang was the first emperor of China, and the army was made to keep him company when he died. Each statue is unique, so it makes the warriors look like a real army. My favorite thing about the story is that the army wasn't discovered until 1973. Some farmers were digging to make a well on their lands when they came across the artifacts. Of course, archaeologists wanted to find out more so they bought the land from the farmers, six of whom were brothers. Some of the brothers decided to work in the Terracotta Warrior museum, and they signed books and worked in the gift shop. Imagine what else is hiding under the ground, waiting to be discovered.

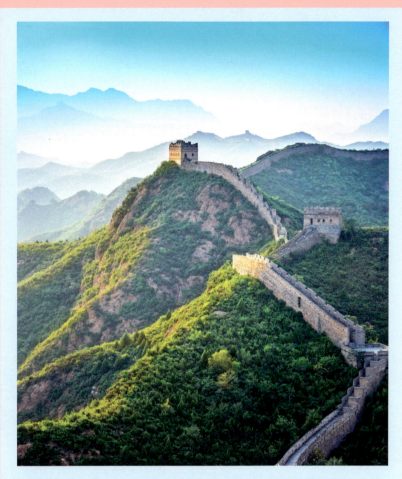

Emperor Qin Shi Huang is also famous for another Chinese artifact, which people say you can see from space. Do you know what it is? It's the Great Wall of China, which in Chinese we call Chang Cheng. He didn't start the wall, but he joined together the bits that earlier rulers had made and made it longer. Over the years, different leaders repaired and made changes to the wall, and people built the most famous parts during the Ming Dynasty.

Fun Fact

In the 1400s, China invented a brush with bristles for cleaning teeth.

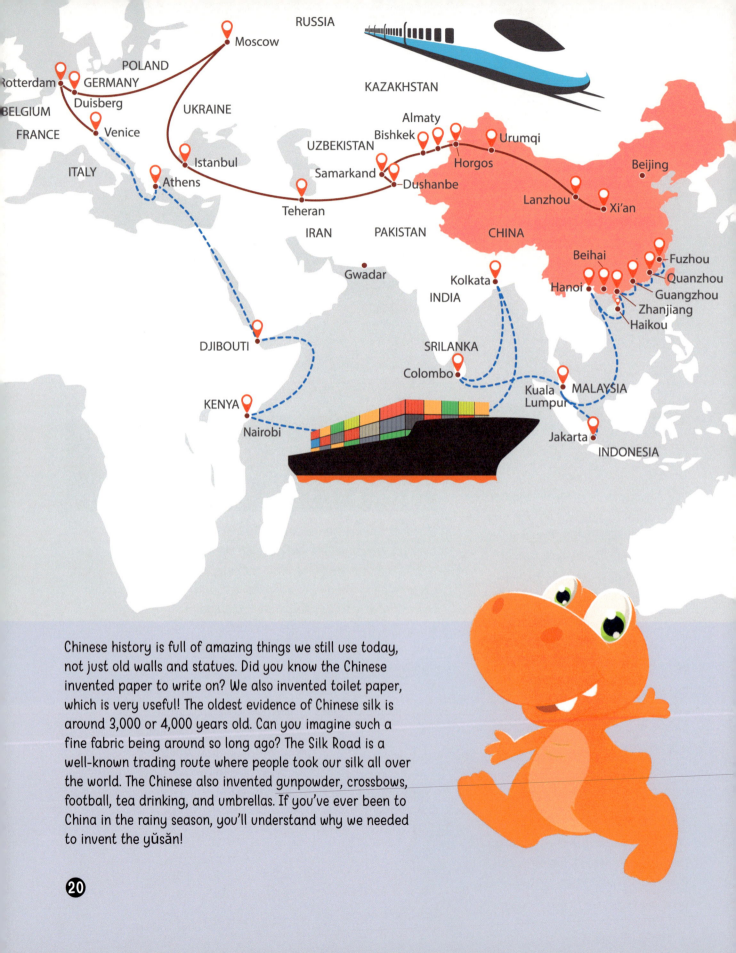

Chinese history is full of amazing things we still use today, not just old walls and statues. Did you know the Chinese invented paper to write on? We also invented toilet paper, which is very useful! The oldest evidence of Chinese silk is around 3,000 or 4,000 years old. Can you imagine such a fine fabric being around so long ago? The Silk Road is a well-known trading route where people took our silk all over the world. The Chinese also invented gunpowder, crossbows, football, tea drinking, and umbrellas. If you've ever been to China in the rainy season, you'll understand why we needed to invent the yŭsăn!

Different emperors and dynasties wanted to take control, so there have been a lot of battles. In modern history, China hasn't had an easy time either. When the last dynasty of China ended (the Qing Dynasty, in 1911) China became a republic, and Sun Yat-sen formed the Chinese National Party.

Later, Mao Zhedong formed the Chinese Communist Party. The Communist Revolution was a war in China, and many people died. Mao Zhedong didn't like traditional parts of Chinese culture and tried to modernize the country. Perhaps he thought he was doing a good thing, but it turned out to be bad. Students and young people joined the Red Guards, and they were encouraged to attack older people.

Dr Sun Yat-sen Memorial Hall, Guangzhou, China

Mao died in the 1970s, and while some older people in China still respect him, younger people know that he was a tyrant and a dictator. In modern China, things are different. We don't have an emperor now, and our country has seen rapid changes in recent decades. Foreigners like to visit and live in China, which wasn't always allowed in the past.

Fun Fact:

Mao thought that sparrows were a pest (along with rats, flies, and mosquitoes) and encouraged people to kill the birds. But when the birds were dead, nothing was left to eat the insects, so the insects ate the grain, and people had nothing to eat. In the Great Chinese Famine that followed, between 15 million and 45 million people died. This goes to show the importance of ecological balance.

Pop Quiz!

When was the Tang Dynasty in China?

1. 221 - 206 BC
2. 960 - 1279 AD
3. 618 - 906 AD

(Answer — 3 (618 AD. 221 - 206 BC was the Qin Dynasty, and 960 - 1279 AD was the Song Dynasty)

Our economic development means that while many Chinese people are still very poor and work in the countryside as they have always done, in big cities many people are very rich and have luxuriant lifestyles. I think my family is somewhere in the middle. My Yéyé had a traditional job and worked hard, but my father works in a city and can earn a lot. I want to have a good future and have enough money to live well, but I don't want to be greedy, and I never want to forget the traditional values and customs of my Chinese heritage.

CHAPTER 4
NATIVE ANIMALS AND PLANTS

Nǐ hǎo, péngyǒu! That's how you say 'hello friend' in Chinese. One of my best friends is my cat, who was a kitten when I was a baby, but she's quite old and frail now. My cat's name is BaoBao, because she's so fat! Even when she was a kitten she had a round little belly. Actually, her name is Baozi, which is the name of a popular Chinese snack. Baozi are steamed buns with delicious fillings, and when BaoBao has eaten her dinner, she looks like a little dumpling herself!

It's nice to see a fat kitty cat because there are a lot of thin, dirty stray cats in China. My best friend found and adopted a kitten. The little cat looked grey but under all the dirt its fur was actually white. He called her Snowy, but he wasn't allowed to keep her, so Snowy went to live with his cousin instead.

Fun Fact:
The biggest zoo in China is Beijing Zoo, which has over 14,0000 animals living there.

China has a strange relationship with animals. Most Chinese people wouldn't understand what I mean by that, but if you've been to foreign countries, you know that China isn't the best place to be an animal. China is well-known for its cruelty to animals, and if you go to the zoo here it's usual to see animals in very small cages, with no grass or natural surroundings. In some zoos, they make animals do tricks. My school took me to the zoo, and we saw some brown bears who had to ride on roller skates and ride a bike.

Then there were some pigs that they made jump off a diving board into a little pool of water. Everyone else was laughing, but I knew it wasn't good. The animals were sad and didn't like it. But it's part of our culture, and it's very difficult to change these things when people have done them for so long.

Can you guess what the national animal of China is? I'll give you some clues. It's black and white and eats bamboo. It's the symbol of the World Wide Fund for Nature, which is a charity that helps a lot of animals. This animal is usually quite slow and lazy and likes to sleep, but in the morning the little ones play. Can you guess? It's the giant panda! In Chinese, we call it the Da XiongMao, which means big bear cat. Actually, it used to be the other way around. Pandas were called MaoXiong (cat-bear), but then the Chinese writing system changed, and everyone called it the Xiong-Mao (bear-cat). So they decided to change it so that nobody would be confused.

In Chengdu, there is a really great place to see pandas. It's a zoo, but it's not like a normal Chinese zoo. The pandas are treated really well and have a lot of trees to climb and a big space to run around in. It's called the Chengdu Research Base for Giant Panda Breeding. Pandas need help because they're not very good at having babies, so they are a vulnerable species, although they're not endangered as much as they were before. Mummy pandas are quite clumsy and because a baby panda is so small, sometimes the baby gets lost or sat on! It sounds funny but it's quite sad, and I'm glad that the zoo in Chengdu has been so successful in helping the pandas survive.

Although the giant panda is the most famous, it's not the only special animal we have in China. There are lots of breeds of dog that come from China, such as the Chow Chow, Shih Tzu, Pekingese, and Pug. In my opinion, most of the dogs from China are small and silly. I like 'proper' dogs that look like wolves; dogs that you can play games with and not just put in your handbag! The Kunming Wolfdog is my favorite, and they are so clever. They can be trained to work with firemen or policemen, and sometimes they are used by the military. I'd really like a Kunming Wolfdog for a pet, and I'd call him Hero. But Māmā says I can't have one until I'm old enough to look after it and to pay for its food myself.

Fun Fact:

Half of the time, mummy pandas have twins. In the wild, only one of the twins will survive, but in captivity it's more likely that both twins will live.

Some types of animals in China are really endangered, or maybe they are extinct already but nobody knows because we see them so rarely. One of these is the white dolphin, which we call baiji. Do you think dolphins always live in the ocean? Well, our white dolphins live in a river called the Yangtze River. But now, the river is dirty, and we haven't seen the white dolphin for a long time, so some people think it's died out. I hope the baiji swam to some secret place where there are no humans, and it can live safely.

White Dolphins

Fun Fact: Sometimes the white dolphin turns pink.

Once when I went to a zoo, I discovered a cool story about Pere David's deer. These deer were native to China, and while they are now extinct in the wild and only live in zoos, it's really amazing that they didn't die out altogether. The deer belonged to the Tongzhi, the Emperor of China in the 19th century. In 1895, there was a big flood, and the wall that kept the deer in the royal garden fell down, and deer escaped. But they weren't free, because at that time many people in China were poor and starving. The peasants captured the special deer and ate them, and then there were only about 30 left.

A few years later, there was a battle called the Boxer Rebellion when soldiers went into the palace, and they killed all the rest of the deer, so there were none left. So everyone thought that the deer were extinct. But then people discovered that, some years earlier, someone had illegally taken some of the Pere David's deer out of China, and there was a rich man in England named Herbrand Russell who had some in his garden. Because of him, the deer survived and can now be seen in zoos, although they don't live in the wild anymore. The deer are named after a French missionary who came to China in the mid 1800s. What an amazing story!

Ginkgo biloba tree in diminishing perspective in the fall

The national flower of China is the plum blossom, which we call méihuā. I like plum blossoms more than cherry blossoms, which is popular in Japan. The plum blooms have a darker color and appear earlier in the year. Our national tree is the ginko, which everyone relates to Japan but is popular in China too.

And while a kiwi might make you think of New Zealand, the fuzzy kiwi is actually the national fruit of China. I think that's weird because we have some many other special types of fruit in China that they could have chosen instead.

China has a broad range of flora and fauna (which means wildlife, both plants and animals) because the country is so diverse. Some places are hot and sunny while others are cold and dry. We have monsoons and rainy seasons, and our land varies from flat plains to soaring mountains. The population of China grows and grows, and we've taken over a lot of space that wildlife used to enjoy and have all to themselves. But still I think China is a very wild country.

There are places you can go where there are no people and where there are secrets yet to be discovered.

Fun Fact

Frangipani is a flower native to Thailand and isn't very popular in China. Both Peony and Orchid flowers grow well in China and have important meanings.

CHAPTER 5
FOOD, CULTURE, AND TRADITIONS

Culture is a funny thing. I think the hardest thing to understand about a country's culture and traditions is that you never really understand your own culture until you visit somewhere else. If you've only spent time in one place your whole life, everything seems normal to you. But it's when you go somewhere new, and you realize you do things differently, that you can see how places have such varied cultures and traditions.

Chinese people have difficulty understanding this because so few of us get to go abroad. A lot of people in China are still very poor and can't afford to go on holiday to other countries. Even people who are quite rich don't get to go away often because it's so expensive, and China isn't very close to places that most people want to go to. Most Chinese tourists go to other places in Asia because it's closer to travel to and cheaper as well. Far fewer tourists from China go to Europe or America.

Fun Fact:
The Chinese New Year is the biggest human migration on Earth, when around 3 billion trips take place.

But on the plus side, one thing about Chinese people not traveling much and our society being insular is that we have a strong identity with important traditions that haven't gone out of fashion over the years. In countries with a cosmopolitan population of people from different places, the culture has mixed influences and changes into something new. However, in China our traditions haven't changed so much.

Family is really important in China. Spending time with your relatives is more important than spending time with friends, and in China people often live in big families. Children, parents, grandparents... all living under one roof. We look after each other, and families always meet up when it comes to important holidays. Things have changed a little these days because young people want to move away from their families and live in big cities to work in offices. However, when people get married and have children, they might move back home. Also, wherever they are, Chinese people always go home for the Chinese New Year!

I'm lucky because I already live with my grandparents, so we don't have to travel during the festival. Sometimes our other relatives come and visit us instead, and there are so many of them that we don't have room for them all. Some of them have to rent a room in a hotel.

My best friend has family living in Tibet, and sometimes he travels there for their traditional reunions. It's a long journey, and I don't envy him!

Pop Quiz!

Which of these Chinese words means spoon?

1. Kuàizi
2. Pánzi
3. Sháozi

(Answer – 3. Sháozi means spoon. Kuàizi are chopsticks, and a dnzi is a plate.)

When you visit a foreign country, it's important to learn about the traditions so you don't offend anyone. Māmā said that she learned this very quickly when she went to study in England. In China, we think it's rude to blow your nose into a tissue, but in England, everybody does that all the time. At first Māmā thought it was so disgusting, but then she learned to be tolerant of their way of life. In China, it's customary to spit on the floor but in many countries it's rude to do that, so when Chinese people go abroad, they have to watch their manners!

Fun Fact:
Chinese chopsticks are called kuàizi, and it's bad luck to use two sticks that are different lengths.

If you ever come to China, be careful when you are eating food, because it's easy to offend a Chinese person by eating in the wrong way. For example, don't ever stab your chopsticks upright in a bowl of rice. We think that this makes the chopsticks look like the incense sticks we burn at a funeral, so please don't stab your chopsticks into your rice! Also, you shouldn't stab your food with your chopsticks. Even if something is tricky to pick up, chopsticks are only used for grabbing or scooping food. It's rude to push your chopstick inside something like a dumpling. If you can't manage to grab your food with chopsticks, use a spoon instead.

There are so many things you need to learn to be polite in China. For instance, if you offer a Chinese person a gift, we think its polite to refuse the gift one time before accepting it. So if you try to give someone a present and they say "No," don't just take it back! You should offer it one more time to see if they were just being polite. Also, be careful when you compliment someone in China. If you tell a Chinese person that you really like something of theirs, like their jewelry, they might take it off and try to give it to you as a gift! So rather than saying "I really like your jade necklace," it might be better to say, "That jade necklace really suits you."

In China, our ceremonies are very important and we like to maintain old traditions. On her wedding day, a Chinese bride won't wear a big white dress like people wear in the Western world. A traditional Chinese wedding dress will be a qipao dress, which is a slim, well-fitting dress and for a wedding it will be red, often with beautiful golden designs on it. The bride also wears a red veil.

But now in modern times, a lot of Chinese brides want more than one dress. They want to have a traditional Chinese red qipao, and a white western dress, and sometimes they have a third dress to wear to the party in the evening! I feel sorry for the family of the bride because it must be so expensive to host a wedding in China!

Fun Fact:

Three days after a wedding in China, the couple will visit the family of the bride. She is no longer a part of that family because she has joined her husband's family, and so this is an important visit to show that they are still welcome in her house.

It may seem like there are lots of risks in coming to China because there are so many important cultural differences you need to be aware of, but you shouldn't worry. Chinese people have a good sense of humor, so if you make a mistake, just apologize, and it will be okay. For a good guide, copy what Chinese people are doing. Also, if you aren't sure what to do, ask a Chinese person for advice, because Chinese people love to be teachers and give information to foreigners.

People celebrate in different ways when it's their birthday. How are birthdays celebrated in your country? Do you know anything about birthdays in China?

All over the world, it has become customary to eat a birthday cake on your special day. However, in China there is another food we must eat, which is a bowl of birthday noodles! But these are no ordinary noodles. On our birthday, we eat longevity noodles, which are special because they are really, really long. Eating long noodles symbolizes a long and healthy life, so we Chinese eat them each year on our birthdays to bring us good luck. Sometimes people have just one noodle, and it's so long that it fills the bowl, and you have to slurp it all in one go and not break it!

Hey, it's Chen here! I hope you're having a wonderful day. I'm really happy because tomorrow is my birthday! I'll be twelve years old, which means that soon it will be time for me to start secondary school, so it's an important landmark.

Fun Fact:

Certain ages are seen to be unlucky in China, such as 30, 33 and 66 for women, and 40 for men. When they reach this milestone, they won't celebrate it or acknowledge it until the following year, when they add two years to their age, so they can miss the unlucky number!

By the way, my real age is twelve, but everybody says it's my thirteenth birthday. We calculate birthdays differently in China, so that when a baby is born, he or she is already one year old! But because my Māmā has lived abroad and knows about foreign customs, she doesn't believe in using my Chinese age. Traditions are hard to break in China, and so my Nainai and Yéyé will say 'Happy Thirteenth Birthday!' instead.

One of the most important national holidays in China is the Chinese New Year. While most of the world celebrates New Year on January 1st, in China we celebrate it according to the lunar calendar, and it usually happens in early February. Each year has a different animal called the Chinese Zodiac Animals. The year you are born in, and the characteristics of that animal, are said to predict what kind of person you will be.

We also call this celebration the Spring Festival, and everyone travels to be with their families. On the main day of the festival, our skies are aflame with wonderful firework displays. The translation of our word for fireworks means 'fire flower,' which I think is beautiful. Next time you see some fireworks, you'll see what I mean, because they look like giant flowers blooming in the sky. Visitors enjoy the Spring Festival Temple Fair at Ditan Park, for the celebrations of the chinese New Year.

For Chinese New Year, we put up a lot of decorations in red and gold. These are our lucky colors, and people believe they bring happiness and good luck. We also give presents, or at least, older people give presents to the children in their family. I'm lucky because I'm the only child, so I get all the presents. Actually, we don't give presents but money, which is always given in a red envelope.

Another important Chinese holiday is the Tomb Sweeping Festival, which happens in April. On this day, we visit the tombs of our ancestors, clean them up, and spend time praying and thinking about our ancestors. Some of my classmates visit the tombs of their grandparents, but because my grandparents are young, they're still alive, so I'm lucky.

Girl sits and pays respect at the grave of her family during the Chen Ming Festival

Fun Fact
20% percent of the world's population celebrates Chinese New Year. Chinese New Year isn't just celebrated in China, but all over the world where Chinese and Asian people live.

We visit the graves of my great-grandparents, and of my grandfather's brother, who died before I was born. One of my favorite festivals is the Mid Autumn Festival, which happens in September or October. We eat mooncakes, which are round pastries with a sweet bean paste filling. They have pretty pictures printed in the top and sometimes come in different shapes. Mooncakes can be very expensive, and people give big boxes of them as presents. During this festival, we also decorate the streets with lanterns that attract the fireflies.

Christmas isn't really a big deal in China. Of course, in modern times we celebrate it like the rest of the world does, and children get some presents too, but it's not our most important festival. Actually, across China, most people don't celebrate Christmas at all. If you live in a big city, it's more likely you'll celebrate Christmas because of all the commercial things and advertising. If you live in a village, you probably won't do anything special at all. Most Chinese people still go to work on Christmas Day. But because my mother got used to enjoying Christmas when she was in England, she has continued the tradition here. Oh, and we don't eat a roast dinner with turkey. At Christmastime, it's traditional to eat an apple, because it symbolizes love and good luck!

Fun Fact:

When Chinese people give someone a gift, like a red envelope, they always present it to them in two hands, not just one hand.

Another favorite festival of mine is the Dragon Boat Festival. I already told you that Lishui, the place where I live, is famous for its water. During the Dragon Boat Festival, it's great fun to go and watch the dragon boat races on the lakes. One day I'd love to take part in a dragon boat race, but I need to wait until I'm bigger and stronger and can practice the skills needed to win. During this festival, we eat zongzi, which are triangles of rice wrapped up in a bamboo leaf with a savory filling.

Fun Fact

Dragon Chinese zodiac animal is the most popular zodiac sign in China. Lots of couples in China try to have a baby in the dragon year, and many more babies are born in the dragon years than other years. The goat is thought to be the unluckiest of the zodiac signs.

Năinai is preparing a big meal because it's a Saturday which means all five of us will be together. Right now, Yéyé is down at the lake fishing. I wanted to go with him but, unlucky for me, I have too much homework to do. Hopefully he will bring back a big fish which we can eat at the feast! Steamed fish with ginger and spring onions is one of my favorites… yum!

So we are waiting for Yéyé, but also for Māmā who is traveling back home on the train, and Bàbà has gone to meet her at the train station. Family meals are nice, but I don't want to wait for food!

> **Fun Fact:**
> In China, the most popular meat is pork.

"Āiyā, my stomach is grumbling. I'm so hungry! Don't you just hate it when you want to eat something and lunch isn't ready yet?"

Māmā told me that when she was studying in England, she was really surprised because the three daily meals are so different. Breakfast has types of food that most people will only eat in the morning, like cereal. Lunch is often cold and small if people take it to work or school, but it's usually bigger and hot on the weekend, especially if you have 'Sunday lunch.' Dinner is the biggest meal and is usually hot. For me, this is so strange. In China, we don't really separate breakfast, lunch, and dinner. You can eat any type of food at any time of day.

In China, very few people are vegetarian. Usually, people are vegetarian if they are Buddhists, but I think even they would eat meat if they could. In the past, China was a very poor country and people didn't have a lot to eat, especially meat. Now that most people are richer, they want to have meat with every meal.

We have two staples in China which are rice and noodles. You might have heard of the 'rice line' or 'wheat line.' In China, people in the South grow a lot of rice, so they eat it every day. But in North China, the climate and temperature are different, so it's better for them to grow wheat. In the North, people like to eat a lot of things they can make with wheat, such as noodles and bread. In the past, the rice line showed a big difference in the daily diet of the population. These days, transporting things is easier, so we can eat whatever we want, but our growing traditions stay the same.

I prefer rice over noodles. Maybe that's because I'm in the South! I like rice because it soaks up all the flavors of whatever you're eating. In other countries, people think that the Chinese are crazy to use chopsticks for something as small as rice. But of course, we don't pick up the rice one grain at a time! Actually, we usually scoop up a clump of rice, as if the chopsticks were a spoon. It's easy once you practice.

Fun Fact:

If you've had a 'Chinese Take-out' in your country, it's probably quite different to the real Chinese food you get in mainland China. Many Chinese people who set up Chinese restaurants abroad are actually from Hong Kong, so the cooking is not Chinese style, but Cantonese style.

Fun Fact:

Chinese children sometimes use 'training chopsticks' which are stuck together so you can't drop one of them.

Century Egg

I think that people in other countries are surprised when they come to China because we eat things that they find strange. For example, in some places in China you can eat dog meat, but this is a delicacy and expensive. Other meat that we eat in China includes bullfrog, spiders, insects, seahorses, duck head, and more. We don't waste anything!

We love eggs in China, too. There is a special dish called the 100-year-old egg, or century egg. The eggs are preserved and turn a different color after many weeks and months. I don't like the century eggs because they're too chewy and look like jelly. But eggs are a good source of protein and give you energy, so I try to eat at least one egg every day.

Box of Black Deep Fried Stinky Tofu with Red Chili

Another source of protein is tofu, which is made from bean curd. If you're a vegetarian, you'll eat a lot of tofu in China! One popular dish is called chòudòufu, which means stinky tofu. The smell is really overwhelming, and if someone is cooking it on the street, you can smell it from miles away! But I think you should really try it. The smell is disgusting but, trust me, the taste is good! It's just like strong cheese.

Each region in China has a different cuisine. Sichuan Cuisine is famous because it's so spicy. One famous dish is Kung Pao chicken, and another is spicy hot pot. The hot pot bowl has room for two different types of soup. The red soup is hot and spicy, and the white soup is cooler. Don't mix the two types together, or everything will taste spicy.

Hot pot soup

Pop Quiz!

Which type of Chinese cuisine does Chow Mein (stir-fried noodles) come from?

1. Cantonese cuisine
2. Sichuan cuisine
3. Fujian cuisine

(Answer 1 — Cantonese cuisine. Like dumplings and spring rolls, stir-fried noodles come from the Hong Kong area. Sichuan cuisine is famous for spicy dishes, and Fujian cuisine is famous for fresh seafood.)

One of my favorite Chinese dishes is Ma Pour Tofu, which is a tofu dish with a spicy sauce that has beef mince in it. Beijing duck is another favorite of mine because I love rolling the little pancakes with the sweet hoisin sauce, but this dish is often expensive so we don't have it often. From the south, I like to eat dumplings and wontons, especially wonton soup which is great when the weather is cold.

In China, desserts aren't so good. I like chocolate more than anything, but this isn't a Chinese invention. Chinese pudding can be a bit gloopy, and the sweet flavor doesn't come from chocolate but from sweet bean paste. My Nainai likes glutinous rice balls with a black sesame paste inside, but I don't like them because they make my teeth glue together. Moon cakes are nice, but we only have those in the Autumn.

I think I already told you about baozi, right? I named my cat BaoBao after these steamed buns, which are usually savory. But you can also get sweet baozi. I really like the custard baozi, and sometimes you can find a sweet baozi that's shaped like a peach, and has been dyed pink at the top. I'm not a fan of the sweet bean paste baozi, but my friend told me he once had a chocolate baozi — that would be my ideal sweet treat!

Fun Fact

In Summer Chinese people eat a lot of watermelon. Watermelon is refreshing when the weather is hot.

What kinds of Chinese food do you like best? If you haven't tried some before, you're going to enjoy it when you do! Oh, I'm so hungry... but I can hear the front door opening and everyone is coming home, so soon it's time for lunch!

CHAPTER 6
FAMOUS PEOPLE OF CHINA

Do you know many famous people from China? Around the world, people recognize celebrities from places like America, but it's not so common to be familiar with celebs from other cultures. If you had to list some famous Chinese people, I think you'd probably mention political figures like Chairman Mao.

> **Fun Fact**
> Bruce Lee also had a daughter, named Shannon Lee, who is also an actress.

But there are also some famous Chinese actors you might be familiar with. Do you know Bruce Lee? Ok, I know that Bruce isn't a Chinese name. His Chinese name was Lee Jun-fan, and he was what is now called an ABC, which means American Born Chinese. He was born in San Francisco but his parents went back to Hong Kong when he was just a baby. Bruce Lee was born in the year of the dragon (which is the most popular year) and in the hour of the dragon, which means people believe is super lucky.

He must have been lucky to become a successful actor, but he had some help in that regard because his father was in the acting business. Bruce is known for his martial arts and is one of the most famous Chinese actors of all time. But his luck ran out, because Bruce Lee died when he was only 32-years-old, after a bad reaction to some medicine. Many people think that the Lee family was cursed, because Bruce Lee's son also died very young. Brandon Lee was an actor just like his father, and starred in a movie where someone was shooting at him. There was a problem with the gun they were using in the scene. It was only supposed to pretend to shoot, but Brandon Lee was actually shot and died soon after. Because both Bruce and Brandon Lee died when they were young, there are lots of conspiracies about this, and it has probably made them even more famous.

A famous Chinese actor who is still alive today is Jackie Chan. His Chinese name is Chan Kong-sang, and he was born in Hong Kong. When Jackie Chan was a boy, his nickname was Paopao, which means cannonball, because he was so energetic and always running around everywhere! Jackie Chan is really famous and has been one of the most highly-paid actors in the world. But despite his fame, I think he's probably a nice guy because he does a lot for charity. His parents were refugees of the civil war in China and had a really bad life before he was born, so now Jackie Chan does his best to help those in need.

So far, the only famous people I've thought of have been actors, and they've all been men, too! Māmā said that she became a feminist when she went to England, and she always tries to show me examples of inspiring women, not just men. So I actually know about some famous Chinese women too, but you probably haven't heard of them.

One famous Chinese woman of the past was Ching Shih. She wasn't an actress; she was a pirate! Born in 1775, she was in command of more than 300 Chinese sailing ships. If you read about everything she did, it's easy to see why people call her the most successful pirate of all time. Most pirates get captured or killed at some point, but Ching Shih didn't. She lived until she was nearly 70 years old. She must have been a brave woman, but I think she was also a little crazy, because after her husband died she got married to her stepson.

Fun Fact:

Have you seen *The Pirates of the Caribbean* movies? In the third movie, perhaps you'll recognize one of the pirates who looks like an old Chinese woman. It's Ching Shih!

We don't have Emperors in China anymore, but our last emperor ruled not long ago. The last emperor of China was Puyi, the 12th emperor of the Qing dynasty. When he came to the throne as a small boy, the world had changed while China had stayed the same. Traditional life in China couldn't fit in with the modern world, and Puyi had to step down from his role. Actually, he was in prison for a long time and ended his life as a gardener in Beijing. Can you imagine being an Emperor who is so important that you don't even have to brush your own teeth or get dressed by yourself, and then you go to prison where you have to do everything by yourself, and finally you end up working as a gardener? What a crazy life Puyi had!

Fun Fact

Popular Disney story *Mulan* was based on the Chinese legend of Hua Mulan, a warrior who pretended to be a man so she could fight.

Tomb of Empress Dowager Cixi

Actually, just as famous as Puyi is the Empress Dowager Cixi, who chose him as the Emperor after she died. The Empress's own son had died at the age of 18, and he was already the Emperor but everybody knew he would be bad at it. So the Empress kept control until her death, even though that's not how things were normally done in China. But it was a time of change, and of course, it changed even more after her death because Puyi was the last Emperor in Chinese history.

I think I already told you that Chinese history isn't my favorite subject because there is so much to learn, and so many facts and dates that I should memorize. But I'm always interested to read out the stories of people's lives. To me, knowing that Jackie Chan was called 'cannonball' and that the best pirate in China was a woman, those facts are more interesting to me than knowing how many years Chairman Mao was in power, or knowing what date the Great Wall was built. What do you think? Which of the famous Chinese people I've mentioned is the most interesting to you?

CHAPTER 7
MAJOR CITIES AND ATTRACTIONS

Every country in the world has landmarks that it's famous for. These are the places and attractions that first spring to mind when you think of that country. India has the Taj Mahal, France has the Eiffel Tower, The United Kingdom has Big Ben in London, America has the White House, Italy has St Peter's Basilica… what about your country? What are the most famous landmarks in the place you come from?

China has a lot of landmarks, because it is so big and has such a big population, but many foreigners will only be able to tell you about a handful of them. Of course, I think that the Great Wall of China is the most famous one, but what do you actually know about it? Many people think that you can see the wall from space, but this isn't true. Sure, it's a really big wall, but it's not big enough to see from the moon! Here are some true facts about the Great Wall of China:

- It isn't one long wall with a start and a finish. The Great Wall is actually lots of smaller walls that add up to make one big wall.

- The Great Wall is the longest structure people have ever built.

- The oldest parts of the wall are more than 2,000 years old.

- The wall wasn't built all by the same Emperor and different rulers added to it to over time.

- You can a marathon run along the Great Wall. It's been running since 1999 and is one of the most challenging marathons that you can do. This small event is for just 2,500 dedicated runners, and they can enjoy the spectacular views when they're running, as long as they are careful not to fall off the wall!

Aerial view of Beijing with historical architecture

Summer Palace in Beijing

When people visit Beijing, which is our capital, the Great Wall isn't the only attraction that people flock to see. Also popular is the Forbidden City. This impressive building was the imperial palace until 1912, when Puyi abdicated, and we didn't have an Emperor again. The palace was built in the 1400's, and in Chinese we call it Zìjìnchéng.

Fun Fact:

It took more than a million workers to complete the Forbidden City.

You might not have heard of some other attractions in Beijing. Similar to the Forbidden City is the Summer Palace, which is a UNESCO World Heritage Site. There were some temples and gardens in that area in the past, and then in the mid 1700s, the Emperor wanted to build a lovely palace as a present to his mother, because it was her 60th birthday. Isn't that a wonderful present? For my Nainai's 60th birthday, all my father bought her was a silk scarf! In the Summer Palace is a building with a long corridor, and it's particularly famous because of the beautiful paintings that are on the wooden beams above your head.

Beijing National Stadium

Also in Beijing, you can visit the buildings from the Beijing Olympics which were held in 2008. The Bird's Nest is the most famous Olympic building. If you like art, you should go to the 798 Art District in Beijing. You can find interesting modern art, including sculptures and graffiti in this cool, funky place.

It's not just Beijing that has nice attractions to visit. The nearest big city to me is Shanghai, which is actually the biggest city in the world. The most famous attraction in Shanghai is The Bund, which we call Wàitān, a famous street that runs next to the river in the city centre. You can look across the water and see some of the most impressive skyscrapers in the world, and behind you on the street there are a lot of famous buildings, too. I like the Pearl Tower best because it has a beautiful shape and the pink color is unusual to see in architecture.

Tiananmen Square is another famous place, but many Chinese people don't know why. In 1989, students protested against the government. The government wasn't happy, and it sent the army to make the people go away, but they refused, and so the army shot a lot of people. People believe around 10,000 people died. But after this happened, the Chinese government wanted people to forget what they had done. They made it impossible for people to find out the truth. When Māmā went to England, British students told her about the Tiananmen Square Massacre. She couldn't believe it at first, and although she has taught me all about it, she said I should talk to other Chinese people about it, because I might get in trouble. China can be a crazy place sometimes! Even today, most Chinese people don't know the truth about Tiananmen.

Oriental Pearl Tower and the Bund at Shanghai

Traditional pavilions in Yuyuan Gardens, Shanghai

The Yuyuan Gardens are my favorite attraction in Shanghai. It's so pretty! Māmā likes to visit the former French Concession because it reminds her of when she was living in Europe. I also like to visit the big museums in Shanghai, such as the Shanghai Museum which has lots of interesting artifacts, and the Science and Technology Museum which is one of the most fun museums I've ever been to. Little museums are popular with foreigners, like the Propaganda Poster Museum and the Jewish Refugees in Shanghai Museum.

Mt. Huangshan in Anhui, China.

My grandparents don't like visiting big cities, so if they want to go on holiday, we usually choose a smaller place that's nearby, or somewhere with beautiful natural attractions to admire. One of my favorite family holidays was going to Huangshan, which in English means the Yellow Mountains. The mountains are in Anhui Province which isn't too far away from where I live, and you can visit it if you have a long weekend. The mountain's summit is at 1,864 m (6,115 ft) high, and it's a difficult climb.

There are different routes you can take to the top. The Eastern Steps are the ones I did with my grandparents, and it took around three hours to climb up the mountain and two hours to climb down. Yéyé told me that the Western Steps are better because the view is much more astonishing, but it takes seven hours to climb up that way! Maybe when I'm older and stronger I'll be able to do that route with my father, but I'm not fit enough yet!

Fun Fact:

Shanghai municipality has a population of more than 26 million people! 150,000 of the people living in Shanghai are foreigners, and most of them are Japanese, America and Korean.

CONCLUSION

Well, that's all from me, Ping Chen, or Ringo, as I prefer to be called! I hope you've enjoyed everything I've told you about China. It's such a crazy place, and you will have a different experience depending on which parts you go to. Different areas in China are really like different countries. Within this one land, we have different languages, climates, infrastructures, cuisines, and traditions. Choosing where to visit in China is a tough decision. On the one hand, you should spend as much time as possible in each place because that's how you'll really get to know somewhere. But on other hand, you should try to visit as many places as possible because they're all so different.

I think one of the most important things to remember is to go with the flow. You might see things that you think are totally bizarre and not know how to react, or you might go to a restaurant that serves things that you find really weird, or even disgusting. You don't have to try everything or do everything, but do please try to be respectful, because we Chinese are very proud of our culture. More than anything, we love to laugh! Try to make friends with us, even if we can't speak English, because most Chinese people will be so pleased to meet you.

Which parts of China did you like the most and why?

_____
_____
_____
_____
_____
_____
_____
_____
_____
_____

What activities did you enjoy most and why?

_____
_____
_____
_____
_____
_____
_____
_____
_____
_____

*I have thoroughly enjoyed this journey through China with you.
Feel free to visit us at www.dinobibi.com and check out our other titles!*

Dinobibi Travel for Kids

Dinobibi History for Kids

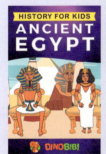 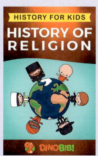   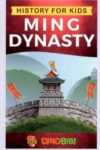
   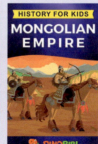 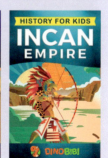

Made in United States
Troutdale, OR
02/01/2024

17295239R00029